Farhana Rashid
Md. Tariqul Islam

Teaching as a profession

Viewpoint of the Bangladeshi
secondary school teachers

Anchor Academic
Publishing

Rashid, Farhana, Islam, Md. Tariqul: Teaching as a profession: Viewpoint of the
Bangladeshi secondary school teachers, Hamburg, Anchor Academic Publishing 2015

Buch-ISBN: 978-3-95489-443-7
PDF-eBook-ISBN: 978-3-95489-943-2
Druck/Herstellung: Anchor Academic Publishing, Hamburg, 2015

Bibliografische Information der Deutschen Nationalbibliothek:
Die Deutsche Nationalbibliothek verzeichnet diese Publikation in der Deutschen
Nationalbibliografie; detaillierte bibliografische Daten sind im Internet über
http://dnb.d-nb.de abrufbar.

Bibliographical Information of the German National Library:
The German National Library lists this publication in the German National Bibliography.
Detailed bibliographic data can be found at: http://dnb.d-nb.de

All rights reserved. This publication may not be reproduced, stored in a retrieval system
or transmitted, in any form or by any means, electronic, mechanical, photocopying,
recording or otherwise, without the prior permission of the publishers.

Das Werk einschließlich aller seiner Teile ist urheberrechtlich geschützt. Jede Verwertung
außerhalb der Grenzen des Urheberrechtsgesetzes ist ohne Zustimmung des Verlages
unzulässig und strafbar. Dies gilt insbesondere für Vervielfältigungen, Übersetzungen,
Mikroverfilmungen und die Einspeicherung und Bearbeitung in elektronischen Systemen.

Die Wiedergabe von Gebrauchsnamen, Handelsnamen, Warenbezeichnungen usw. in
diesem Werk berechtigt auch ohne besondere Kennzeichnung nicht zu der Annahme,
dass solche Namen im Sinne der Warenzeichen- und Markenschutz-Gesetzgebung als frei
zu betrachten wären und daher von jedermann benutzt werden dürften.

Die Informationen in diesem Werk wurden mit Sorgfalt erarbeitet. Dennoch können
Fehler nicht vollständig ausgeschlossen werden und die Diplomica Verlag GmbH, die
Autoren oder Übersetzer übernehmen keine juristische Verantwortung oder irgendeine
Haftung für evtl. verbliebene fehlerhafte Angaben und deren Folgen.

Alle Rechte vorbehalten

© Anchor Academic Publishing, Imprint der Diplomica Verlag GmbH
Hermannstal 119k, 22119 Hamburg
http://www.diplomica-verlag.de, Hamburg 2015
Printed in Germany

Acknowledgement

We are very much grateful to the teachers of selected schools who helped us a lot by giving interviews and providing their opinion. The teachers gave us their valuable times for providing us adequate and valuable data.

We also thankful to different libraries in supplying us essential and suitable books, journals, documents and related thesis paper which helped to enrich our thinking level and the quality of the study.

Finally, we would like to express gratitude many of my teachers, friends and family members for their support and collaboration during this study.

Farhana Rashid
and
Md. Tariqul Islam

Table of Contents

Contents	Page
Acknowledgement	i
Table of Contents	ii
List of Abbreviations	iv
List of Tables	v
List of Figures	vi
Preface	vii

Chapter 1

Introduction	**1-11**
1.1 Background of the study	1
1.2 Objectives of the study	7
1.3 Significance of the study	7
1.4 Operational definition of used terms	9

Chapter 2

Review of Related Literature	**12-22**
2.1 Review of Teaching Profession	12
2.2 Review of Related Research	17

Chapter 3

Methodology	**23-27**
3.1 Nature of the study	23
3.2 Area of the study	24
3.3 Sample of the study	24
3.4 Description of tools	25
3.5 Data collection procedure	26
3.6 Techniques of data analysis	26
3.7 Limitations of the study	27

Chapter 4
Data Analysis and Interpretation **28-45**

Chapter 5
Findings and Discussion **46-56**
5.1 Findings 46
5.2 Discussion 54

Reference **57-63**

List of Abbreviations

B.A	Bachelor of Arts
B.Ed	Bachelor of Education
B.Sc	Bachelor of Science
B.S.S	Bachelor of Social Science
C-in-Ed	Certificate in Education
M.A	Master of Arts
M.Com	Master of Commerce
B.Com	Bachelor of Commerce
SBA	School Based Assessment
BDT	Bangladeshi Taka
M.Ed	Master of Education
M.Sc	Master of Science
M.S.S	Master of Social Science
MCEETYA	Ministerial Council on Education, Employment, Training and Youth Affairs
MS	Micro Soft
SCCT	Social Cognitive Career Theory
SPSS	Statistical Package for Social Science
TQI	Teaching Quality Improvement

List of Tables

Tables	Page
Table 3.1: Study Area	24
Table 3.2: Sampling Design	24
Table 4.1: Influence to involve in teaching and Specialty of teaching profession	29
Table 4.2: Effective and Taken Measures for Students good result	34
Table 4.3: Relation with birth place and carrying out responsibilities out of school	39
Table 4.4: Factors of school environment	40
Table 4.5: Scope of professional development	42

List of Figures

Figures	Page
Figure 2.1: Framework for Professional Standards for Teachings career dimensions and professional elements	15
Figure 4.1: Teaching profession is the best profession	30
Figure 4.2: Factors of teaching profession	30
Figure 4.3: Teachers' view on specialty of Social Science teaching and major subject of teaching	31
Figure 4.4: Enjoyment of Social Science teaching and way of expressing specialty	32
Figure 4.5: Average classes should be conducted for effective teaching	33
Figure 4.6: Helpful and received training for teaching Social Science	34
Figure 4.7: Taking necessary measures for good results in social science	35
Figure 4.8: Opinion about teaching aids and instructional materials	36
Figure 4.9: Students' evaluation methods in social science	36
Figure 4.10: Opinion about effective teaching and assessment	37
Figure 4.11: Roles 'out of school' and 'types of cooperation' to play role	38
Figure 4.12: Support from school administration	41
Figure 4.13: Importance and satisfaction for salary	42
Figure 4.14: Satisfaction in teaching profession as a Social Science teacher	43
Figure 4.15: Mean of teachers' opinion about teaching profession	44
Figure 4.16: Satisfaction of Social Science teachers	45

Preface

Teachers play an important role in fostering the intellectual and social development of children during their formative years. The education that students acquire is the key to determining the future of those students. Secondary school teachers help students investigate more deeply into subjects introduced in primary school and expose them to more information about the world. Secondary school teachers specialize in a specific subject, they also may teach subjects that are career oriented. Additional responsibilities of secondary school Social Science teachers may include career guidance and job placement, as well as following up with students after graduation. Social Science teachers are working in a society loaded with social, environmental and economic problems. So it is very important to know whether Social Science teachers are happy or not in their profession; is they are facing any problem to do their real job; are they making effective citizen for the community and the world.

The purpose of this study was to find out the key aspects of Social Science teachers' profession in Bangladesh and the specialty of teaching Social Science at secondary schools. Understanding the importance of Social Science teachers' perception for their profession the study tried to investigate their perception about the profession. The study concerned a mixed approach. Both qualitative and quantitative data collection and analysis mode were used to investigate teachers' perception regarding their profession. The data findings were presented in statistical and descriptive manner considering various aspects of teaching profession. The study was carried out purposively in 10 schools of Dhaka and Gazipur district. As the study investigated Social Science teachers' professional perception; key issues like training, initiatives for students' results, teaching aids and materials, students' achievement evaluation, responsibility, school environment, school administration, scope and their professional opportunities etc. were discussed with the teachers. In order to maintain the validity of data two types of data collection instruments were used to examine the perception of secondary school Social Science teachers about their profession. In each tool factors related with teachers' role, opportunity, satisfaction and dissatisfaction were set to find out their real view.

Among the interviewed teachers one-third involved in teaching profession from the necessity of job. As teaching profession is not only an occupation but has a great responsibility to the society, concern authority should take proper initiative to encourage qualified young generation to take this profession form its expectation not only for necessity of job. Main reasons for dissatisfaction in teaching profession Social Science teachers mentioned work load, insufficient in-service training, low income, less respect in the society, restriction to use appropriate teaching methods and aids, insufficient library, inadequate preservation system of teaching aids, small classroom, unequal attitude of school administration, political interfere, colleague relation and electricity problem. So schools should increase scopes of professional development for Social Science teachers and proper initiative should be taken to ensure teachers professional satisfaction through salary and other facilities. To encourage teachers to improve their teaching quality, professional qualification and other qualities should be evaluated and provision should be taken to provide better facilities for those, who hold better Degree.

Chapter One

Introduction

1.1 Background of the study

Profession is an occupation that requires considerable training and specialized study. Classically, there were only three professions: Divinity, Medicine, and Law (Perks, 1993). With the rise of technology and occupational specialization in the 19th century, other bodies began to claim professional status: Pharmacy, Logistics, Veterinary Medicine, Nursing, Teaching, Librarianship, Optometry and Social Work, all of which could claim to be professions by 1900 (Buckley & Buckley, 1974). A profession arises when any trade or occupation transforms itself through the development of formal qualifications based upon education and examinations, the emergence of regulatory bodies with powers to admit and discipline members, and some degree of monopoly rights (Bullock & Trombley, 1999). A profession is a vocation founded upon specialized educational training, the purpose of which is to supply disinterested counsel and service to others, for a direct and definite compensation, wholly apart from expectation of other business gain (Statesman, 1917).

Within the family or the society, teaching may be carried out informally. On the other hand, formal teaching may be carried out by salaried professionals. These professionals enjoy a status in some developed societies on a same level with physicians, lawyers, engineers, and accountants. In pedagogy, teachers facilitate student learning or achievement, often in a school or maybe in out of school. But a teacher who teaches on an individual basis may be defined as a tutor.

The teaching profession is a relatively new one. Traditionally, parents, elders, religious leaders, and sages were responsible for teaching children how to behave and think and what to believe. Germany introduced the first formal criteria for the education of teachers in the 18th century. In the 19th century, as society became more industrialized, the concept of schooling became more universal. In industrialized nations today, most teachers are university graduates (Britannica). In Education 'teaching' is a relationship which is established among three focal points- the teacher, the student and the subject matter. The teacher brings the students and the subject matter together through teaching process. Modern teaching is not 'telling and testing' but the complex art of guiding students through a variety of selected experiences towards the attainment of appropriate teaching-learning goals. Teaching is a tri-polar process involving the source of teaching (human and material), students and set of activities designed and manipulated primarily to bring suitable change in the behavior of the students. Functions of teaching are creating learning situations, motivating the child to learn, arranging for conditions which assist in the growth of the child's mind and body, utilizing the initiative and play urges of the children to facilitate learning, turning the children into creative beings, inspiring children with the nobility of thoughts, feelings and actions, giving information and explaining it, diagnosing learning problems, making curricular material and finally evaluating, recording and reporting (Aggarwal, 2005).

Teachers play an important role in fostering the intellectual and social development of children during their formative years. The education that students acquire is key to determining the future of those students. Whether in primary or secondary schools or in private or government schools, teachers provide the tools and the environment for their students to develop into responsible adults. Teachers act as facilitators, using classroom presentations or individual instruction to help students learn and apply concepts in subjects such as science, mathematics, Social Science and English. They plan, evaluate, and assign lessons; prepare, administer, and grade tests; listen to oral presentations; and maintain classroom discipline. Teachers observe and evaluate a student's performance and potential. They are increasingly asked to use new assessment methods. For example, teachers may examine a portfolio of a student's artwork or writing in order to judge the student's overall progress. They then can provide additional assistance in areas in which the student needs help. Teachers also prepare grade papers, prepare report cards, and meet with parents and school staff to discuss a student's academic progress or personal problems. Many teachers use a hands-on approach that utilizes props to help children understand abstract concepts, solve problems, and develop critical thinking skills. They also encourage collaboration in solving problems by having students work in groups to discuss and solve the problems together. To be prepared for success later in life, students must be able to interact with others, adapt to new technology, and think through problems logically. Primary school teachers play a vital role in the development of children. What children learn and experience during their early years can shape their views of themselves and the world and can affect their later success or failure in school, work, and their personal lives. Primary school teachers introduce children to mathematics, language, science, and social studies. They use games, music, artwork, films, books, computers, and other tools to teach basic skills. Secondary school teachers help students investigate more deeply into subjects introduced in primary school and expose them to more information about the world. Secondary school teachers specialize in a specific subject, such as English, mathematics, Social Science, or biology. They also may teach subjects that are career oriented. Additional responsibilities of secondary school Social Science teachers may include career guidance and job placement, as well as following up with students after graduation. In addition to conducting classroom activities, teachers oversee study halls and homerooms, supervise extracurricular activities, and accompany students on field trips. They may identify students who have physical or mental problems and refer the students to the proper authorities. Secondary school teachers occasionally assist students in choosing courses, colleges, and careers. Teachers also participate in education conferences and workshops (Occupational Outlook Handbook, 2010-11).

Many subjects are grouped under the umbrella of Social Science, including history, sociology, civic, economics, population sciences and disaster management. Social Science deals with man, his relation with other men and his environment. It includes that material which is conductive to the development of a well informed, intelligent person who is capable of comprehending properly the current problems, is keen to accept responsibilities as a citizen for the welfare of all and has developed insights, skills and moral qualities which are so essential and desirable in a democratic society (Aggarwal, 1993). The success of education for world wide citizenship depends on the activities of the teacher in general and of the Social Science in particular. The Social Science teacher occupies an essential place in the whole process of Social Science teaching-learning. In spite of the development of modern teaching aids, methods and increasing emphasis on student-centered education, it is still a fact that the teacher can make the subject joyful and effective. Social Science teacher can also inspire and guide the students and create the environment and atmosphere in which training for democratic citizenship becomes possible (Kochhar, 1983).

Around the world teaching profession include the performance of a service to the students, the possession of a unique body of specialized knowledge and technical skill, the requirement of a highly specialized and usually formal preparation, the regulation of standards for the admission to practice by members of the profession and the organization of practitioners into comprehensive professional groups that maintain high standards of conduct and ethics (Gibson, 1965).

Teacher quality has been said to be the number one school-related influence on student achievement. Although research on what constitutes a quality teacher is often the subject of debate, there are some findings on teacher quality that are rarely contested. These suggest that it is what teachers do in classrooms that matters. Research has shown that teachers can improve student achievement when they communicate high expectations, avoid criticism, reward truly praiseworthy behavior, and provide abundant opportunities for success (academic learning time) on material over which students are tested (Waid and Mcnergney, 2003).

Much of the recent research on teacher effectiveness focuses on relating teacher behaviors to student achievement. Quite a bit of the research, however, has delved into stakeholders' perceptions of good teaching—what students, administrators, and teachers themselves think makes an effective teacher. Science suggests that instructional and management processes are keys to effectiveness, but many interview and survey responses about effective teaching emphasize the teacher's affective characteristics, or social and emotional behaviors, more than pedagogical practice. Moreover, the teacher's psychological influence on students has been linked to student achievement in various effectiveness studies (Stronge, 2002).

Local teachers have a different relationship to the community than the other educators in the school where they practice because of their residential history in the neighborhood. Their ties to the community give them a particularized knowledge of the school's social and cultural context and help them to play role out of school. Local teachers know parents, residents, shopkeepers, day care providers, after-school staff, and are acquainted with local institutions, for example, churches, mosques, health care facilities, social service groups, not-for-profit organizations, shopping areas, and so forth. They have an established network of friends and family members and, in many cases, are involved in civic and religious institutions. These all type of responsibility goes to Social Science teachers even they may not be local teacher (Reed, 2009).

Much has been find out about the importance of increasing teacher salaries to attract and retain the brightest and most talented teachers. Many factors have been identified as influencing teacher professional satisfaction and retention, and salary is often at the top of the lists (Michael, 2006). Teachers' perceptions about their school environments, especially in the areas of professional interest and staff freedom, were positively associated with their satisfaction. Several school environmental aspects influenced the total years they planned to teach and their intention to teach at the schools (Huang and Waxman, 2008).

Researches are almost absent in the field of Social Science teachers' perception about their profession in Bangladesh. More study findings are necessary to take initiative for teachers' training, subject based knowledge improvement, salary scheme and school environment. Having recognized the significance of teachers' perception for the development of their profession, the study may show concern personnel and authorities the real situation of the teachers at secondary level for taking time oriented decisions and initiatives.

1.2 Objectives of the study

The specific objectives of the study were as follow:
- To identify the key aspects of teaching profession;
- To know the specialty of teaching Social Science at secondary schools;
- To understand the importance of Social Science teachers' perception for their profession;
- To find out the perception of secondary school Social Science teachers' about their profession.

1.3 Significance of the study

The teacher of Social Science has a responsible role to fill. His tasks are many and varied. He transmits knowledge, directs social research, censors information collected by pupils and may also advise them in choosing their careers and generally act as their guide, philosopher and friend. The teacher of Social Science must become the leader of the local community, its interpreter and reformer. He must be able to transform the school into a center of social reconstruction for a new social order. Educational reforms some times have their beginnings in the class room and some times out of it, but always must they be approved by the teacher and used in the class room before they can take effect. Therefore, the civilization of the future must inevitable look to the teacher of Social Science for much help in the effort to end war before war ends humanity. As a matter of fact, the teacher of citizens of the future is one of the most important agents for promoting good will and preventing chaos (Kochhar, 1983).

Social Science teachers are working in a society loaded with social, environmental and economic problems. The true mission of their profession is making active citizen, they must help their students to learn the value of engaging in long-term efforts to revitalize our democratic society and the skills to respond compassionately to those whose daily needs cannot wait for societal transformation. Social Science teachers are in a unique position to giving their students opportunities for active involvement in the community and the world. So it is very important to know whether Social Science teachers are happy or not in their profession; is they are facing any problem to do their real job; are they making effective citizen for the community and the world (Wade, 1995).

The success of education for world citizenship depends on the daily work of the teacher in general and of the Social Science in particular (Kochhar, 1983). As a great performer for the student as well as for the society Social Science teacher should enjoy their profession. If they are satisfied with their profession they will be able to meet the demand of the students and the society. The study is an effort to understand the perception of Social Science teachers' about their profession. The research focused in various aspects of Social Science teachers' profession. From the study, authority of teachers training college will know the effectiveness of teachers training and its impact on teaching profession. Teachers' thought about class room activities, pedagogical practice and school environment will also find out from professional perception. This information will help the school authority to take initiative for teachers' best performance and satisfaction. Teachers' salary and other facilities are most important issues related with teaching profession. Policy makers and school authority will know the thought of teachers' about their existing facilities from this study to think more about this important profession. Researchers will get opportunities to go ahead from the findings of this research related with teachers training, class room activities, assessment, school environment and teachers' social responsibilities, if teachers are thinking that they need improvement of these fields.

1.4 Operational definition of used terms

Social Science teacher

A teacher works with students and helps them learn concepts in subjects such as science, mathematics, language, Social Science and religion. They then help them apply these concepts (McKay). Social Science teacher deals with attitudes, ideas and appreciations to a large extent than is the case in other branches of study. Social Science demands well prepared conscientious teacher of sound knowledge and training, whose personalities rank high among students. Social Science teacher deals with the teaching of pupils to live together in a democracy and raising the tone of democracy by developing thoughtful, appreciative and an intelligent electorate. Social Science teacher assist pupils to understand this complex world in which we live, in order that this may better adapt themselves to it and prepare themselves for an intelligent and constructive citizenship (Aggarwal, 1993).

Perception

The perception is a process, whereby a meaning is given to a sensation produced by sensory stimulation. It is a means by which a person gains awareness about his/her surroundings and environment. This process helps us to become aware about the world around us. It also indicates about the ability of a person to distinguish an object from its general background. It usually refers to the way, the world looks, tests or smells. The word perception also implies observation, recognition and discrimination. The perception is in a way sensation plus its meaning; it is the basis of knowledge. In fact it is the beginning of knowledge and our sensation gives the raw materials of knowledge and by perception that material is elaborated into definite knowledge of external world. The perception may be subjective or objective. Subjective perception may be faulty at times. Since perception is a component of knowledge; correct knowledge depends on correct perception (Husain, 2004).

Teaching profession

Gibson (1965) examining teaching in the light of major criteria of professional practice find out that, teaching performs a service to the public and requires resources of scientific disciplines, especially psychological and social foundation for its practice. Today's teacher-education programs emphasize general education, education in subjects to be taught and professional education for specialized and formal preparation. Teaching regulates admission to practice by a system of certification and organizes practitioners into comprehensive professional groups that attempt to maintain high standards of conduct and ethics. Considering these criteria (Musgrave, 1979) in twentieth century teaching is an excellent example has come to be known as profession.

Chapter Two

Review of Related Literature

2.1 Review of Teaching Profession

Musgrave (1979) claimed that, a number of characteristics are common to all 'true' professions. These characteristics concern the type of knowledge required to practice, the way in which entry to the professional controlled, the formulation of an ethical code governing professional behavior and finally, the freedom of the professional to practice without lay interference. From the view of Cook and Cook (1960) teaching is a profession in which members acquire a body of systematic knowledge on which their work with people is based, develop an in-group feeling of belonging and responsibility, assume an attitude of moral concern toward students and join together in association to advance the profession, to control member ethics, and so on. Musgrave (1979) found, by the 1970s the status of teaching has risen. This was a result of the fact that education has come to have a higher status, as in the census, amongst those occupation called profession.

The Center for the Future of Teaching and Learning (2009) found that among the teachers secondary school teachers often must do more and do things differently; as a result, they need new and different core understandings and beliefs, content knowledge, pedagogical skills, and professional expertise. Specifically, understanding of the rationale for a given strategy fosters teacher support for implementation. Regardless of which strategies a secondary school is working to adopt, teachers must understand the nature of each strategy and believe in its validity. Teachers' understanding and buy-in are essential because these reforms change their work, often increasing their responsibilities. To make learning more challenging and relevant, secondary school teachers need knowledge of academic or technical subjects and their real-world applications. To implement a given strategy effectively, secondary school teachers need specific pedagogical skills associated with the demands of that strategy. Teachers need additional professional expertise in areas that transcend the classroom to work effectively in secondary schools. Specifically, they need strong interpersonal communication and collaboration skills to work closely with colleagues, industry and higher education partners, and families, and to interact with students in new ways.

Kochhar (1983) suggested that Social Science teacher should have some qualities; i.e. well equipped in academic qualifications, an expert in the methodology of teaching Social Science, a scientist as well as an artist, breadth of outlook and width of understanding, a person of integrity and sound professional ethics and a person who grows professionally.

Raju and Srivastava (1994) presented a need to look at commitment of teachers to their profession in terms of effect, goals and values of the profession. Measuring commitment on this basis, explores the contributing factors and variables to commitment. Empirical evidence on 454 senior secondary school teachers of Delhi, with the help of discriminate analysis, revealed that perceived characteristics of profession, work related personality and desire to improve one's own skills were contributing in that order. The constituent variables that discriminated more and less committed teachers were perceived status, expectations of significant persons, interest in profession, intrinsic motivation, social support, positive group attitudes, perceived advancement and desire to improve skills for professional purpose.

Gonzalez, Brown and Slate (2008) find out some factors that are very important for teachers regarding their profession. These factors are: salary, teacher education program, student discipline, feed back from the school administration and educational resource.

NCEETYA (2003) adopt a National Framework for Professional Standards for Teaching which is an acknowledgement of the need for the highest quality of education to be available to all Australians, and an assurance that this quality should be maintained and built upon for this and future generations. The key to this assurance is the successful partnership between teachers and the teaching profession, teacher educators, teacher employers, the community and Government. The diagram below represents the National Framework for Professional Standards for Teachings career dimensions and professional elements, and illustrates how they interconnect with each other and how they collectively contribute to the central focus of teachers work. The career dimensions and professional elements of the National Framework also provide the factors that are related to the satisfaction or dissatisfaction of their profession.

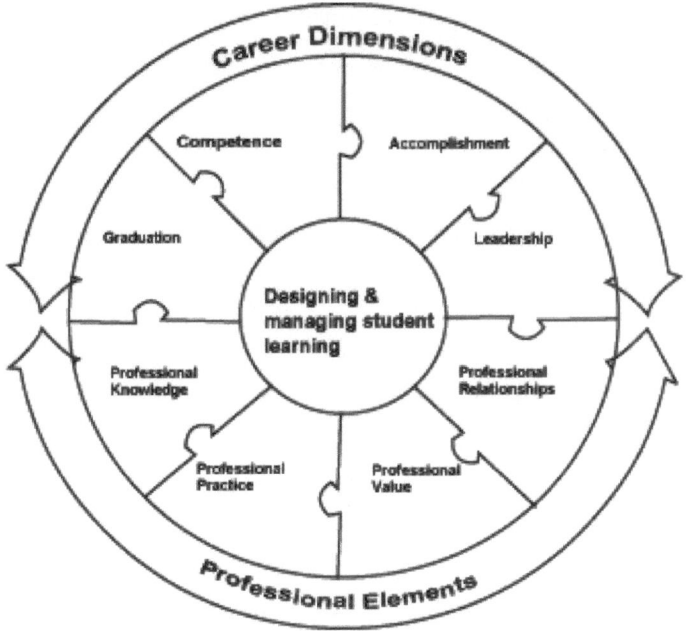

Figure 2.1: Framework for Professional Standards for Teachings career dimensions and professional elements

Career Dimensions

Teachers develop their knowledge, skills and practices throughout their professional lives, but teacher development is not a simple linear process. They enter the profession with varying levels of prior learning, work experience and professional preparation, and work in a range of different contexts. These dimensions do not signify levels of experience; rather they frame general and recognizable aspects of professional capacity and achievement. They reflect a broad continuum of professional development rather than a simple temporal framework of experience. This approach is essentially neither sequential nor lock step and is dependent on application and context. While graduation clearly relates to a specific activity, descriptors of competence, accomplishment and leadership are aspects of professional status, rather than detailed or sequenced events.

Professional Elements

The career dimensions of the National Framework described through specific aspects of teachers work. The categories outlined below have been drawn from a mapping of a range of activities. Professional knowledge related to the teachers fundamental ideas, principles and structure of the disciplines they teach, the links to other content areas and are able to integrate learning across and between content areas, how to effectively teach that content, and the prompts and barriers to learning likely to be encountered by students. Professional practice cover the skills of the teachers to communicate effectively with their students and establish clear goals for learning, to inquiry techniques and teaching strategies, and use a range of tools, activities, and resources to engage their students in learning to organize the content in logical and structured ways to meet learning goals. In Professional values teachers are committed to their own development and continually analyze, evaluate and enhance their professional practice. Professional relationships related within the context that teachers design and manage learning experiences for individuals and groups of students that value opportunities to actively engage with other members of their profession and their wider school communities. This is a relationship that is underpinned by trust, respect and confidence.

2.2 Review of Related Research

According to Oplatka (2007) teaching is characterized in terms of knowledge-transmission, adherence to prescribed curriculum and textbooks, summative assessment of student achievements, and conservativeness. In Chile, teaching is in a period of transition between occupation and profession. To examine teachers' perceptions of their profession, Labrana (2007) conducted a qualitative, phenomenological investigation. He interviewed twenty-seven history and Social Science teachers employed at urban secondary schools in Chile. He found that teachers believe their occupation has the characteristics of a profession, but they perceive that society does not agree with that belief. However, participants reported that their main motivation was to disseminate knowledge to students, not to further the professionalization of their occupation. Labrana (2007) suggests that teachers form a professional organization capable of clarifying and expanding its own body of knowledge. They should also promote classroom activities that stimulate student learning and reasoning beyond the transfer of facts.

Job satisfaction is an important issue, but remains a complex one as it is difficult to measure. Job satisfaction and the teaching profession are highly associated, with an important aspect of quality education and teachers' perception about their profession. A wide range of factors such as the working environment, its manner of organization, demography and individual circumstances, etc., can substantially affect the level of job satisfaction attained by individuals (Saiti, 2007).

Recent national and international studies carried out in a number of countries have drawn attention to the degree of job satisfaction among teachers (Zembylas and Papanastasiou, 2004). In recent years U.S. schools are experiencing teacher shortages, especially in low-income urban areas, because of increased school enrollment, teacher retirement, reduction in class size, teacher attrition, and turnover related to low salaries, job dissatisfaction, and lack of administrative support and influence over decision-making (Gimbert, Cristol, and Sene, 2007). Most of the international studies on teacher satisfaction have been conducted in developed countries, but it is also the need in the available literature for similar research in developing countries as well (Zembylas and Papanastasiou, 2004). Earthman and Lemasters (2009) indicate that the physical environment of school influences attitudes of teachers, which in turn affects their productivity. Such effects could cause morale problems in the teaching staff. They also suggest that school authorities need to recognize the importance physical conditions have upon teachers so that negative feelings and attitudes do not pervade the teacher staff. Such feelings eventually may influence the achievement of students. Cypriot teachers chose this career because of the salary, the hours, and the holidays associated with this profession (Zembylas and Papanastasiou, 2004). Teachers also emphasized their satisfaction with interactions with students, relationships held with colleagues and opportunities to contribute to the growth of individuals and the development of society. Sources of dissatisfaction were social problems and their impact on teachers' work, students' lack of interest and bad behavior, the centralized educational system and the lack of professional autonomy in schools, and teacher evaluation and promotion prospects (Zembylas and Papanastasiou, 2006).

Oplatka (2007) examine the teacher's career in developing countries. Despite the central role of teachers in the social and economic development of their societies, knowledge base of the career of teachers in developing countries is limited and inchoate. He find out that teaching seems to be a kind of default or a supplementary form of income, from which male members seek constantly to escape, and many teachers are described as holding low qualifications with limited opportunities to participate in in-service trainings.

Teachers' professional perception is very much related with their commitment to this profession. Karakus and Aslan (2009) find out that teachers' commitment focuses vary according to their personal characteristics such as gender, marital status and tenure. Keeping in mind the importance of teachers' commitment to various focuses and its effects on school effectiveness, educational leaders should take necessary measures to remedy the troubles which cause teachers' lack of commitment. They find out the need for more supportive and integrative managerial actions to raise teachers' levels of commitment. School leaders may be more concerning and develop special strategies contingent on their employees' personal characteristics to create high commitment workplace.

Liu and Ramsey (2008) examined teachers' satisfaction with various aspects of their job through multilevel analyses of national surveys conducted in the United States. They found that teachers were least satisfied with work conditions and compensation. They also found that teachers' job satisfaction varied with gender, years of teaching, and career status.

On the other hand, Klassen and Anderson (2009) explored the level of job satisfaction and the sources of job dissatisfaction for 210 secondary school teachers in southwest England and compare their results with the results from a similar study published in 1962. Whereas teachers in 1962 were most concerned with external sources of job dissatisfaction (e.g. salary, condition of buildings and equipment and poor human relations), teachers in 2007 expressed the most concern about factors relating to teaching itself (e.g. time demands and pupils' behavior). The changes in sources of dissatisfaction hold true for male and female teachers, with no difference in rankings according to years of teaching experience.

Cerit (2009) examined the effects of servant leadership behaviors of primary school principals on teacher job satisfaction. Strong positive relationship was revealed between servant leadership behaviors of school principals and teachers' job satisfaction and servant leadership was a significant predictor of teacher job satisfaction. Chi Keung (2008) mentioned that teacher Participation in decision-making is one of the recommendations of school-based management and one of the key characteristics of an effective school. The three dimensional decision model includes instructional, curriculum and managerial domains; and the variables of the affective outcome include job satisfaction, job commitment and perception of workload.

Skaalvik and Skaalvik (2009) in their study examined relations between teachers' perception of the school context, teacher burnout, and teacher job satisfaction. Teachers' job satisfaction was directly related to two of the dimensions of burnout (emotional exhaustion and reduced personal accomplishment) and indirectly related to all aspects of the school context, through emotional exhaustion and reduced personal accomplishment. The three dimensions of burnout were differently related to the school context variables. Emotional exhaustion was most strongly related to time pressure whereas depersonalization and reduced personal accomplishment were most strongly related to teachers' relations with parents.

Perrachione, Rosser and Petersen (2008) conducted a study to identify intrinsic and extrinsic variables that influence teacher job satisfaction and retention. The study showed that teachers who experienced satisfaction at their school and/or satisfaction with the profession of teaching were more likely to remain. No relationship was found between satisfaction with the job of teaching, suggesting that retention was determined by teacher satisfaction with the profession and not with work-related duties.

Huysman (2008) analyzed teachers' beliefs and attitudes affecting job satisfaction in one small, rural Florida school district. The majority of rural school teachers rated their overall general job satisfaction as "high." Of the dimensions of job satisfaction the highest ranked factors were all intrinsic satisfaction factors i.e. security, activity, social service, variety, and ability utilization. The lowest ranked satisfaction dimensions were extrinsic satisfaction items which included compensation and school policies, advancement, and recognition. The other items were authority, which was an intrinsic satisfier and considered a non-factor to job satisfaction by the rural respondents, and co-workers, which is a general satisfaction item.

To examine career persistence and job satisfaction of beginning teachers Mau, Wei-Cheng, Ellsworth and Hawley (2008) a job satisfaction model tested using clusters of variables as guided by Social Cognitive Career Theory (SCCT). They found that at the beginning teachers were more satisfied with their jobs than those in other occupations. The social-contextual factors for satisfaction was race, socioeconomic status, teaching license, parents' education, and occupation were among the best predictors of job satisfaction.

Teachers offer consistency in schools and in communities, conveying important messages of stability and societal well-being. Although schools are spread across nations and continents, and school settings vary widely, many of the reasons teachers give for dissatisfaction, which can contribute to teacher absenteeism, are the same the world over: overcrowding of classrooms, poor condition of school buildings, lack of respect for the teaching profession and job stress and burnout. Dealing with such a large-scale global challenge is not easy. Schools must become increasingly creative in finding ways to alleviate teacher stress and improve teaching environments. Teachers' health and well-being must be equally considered alongside other crucial issues of teacher compensation and safe and secure classrooms (Whitehead, 2009).

Chapter Three

Methodology

The purpose of this study was to find out the key aspects of Social Science teachers' profession in Bangladesh and the specialty of teaching Social Science at secondary schools. Understanding the importance of Social Science teachers' perception for their profession the study tried to investigate their perception about the profession. Study nature, area, sample, tools, data collection procedure and techniques of data analysis which are applied to demonstrate the research are described in this chapter.

3.1 Nature of the study

The study concerned a mixed approach. Both qualitative and quantitative data collection and analysis mode were used to investigate teachers' perception regarding their profession. The quantitative approach incorporated a Likert type scale where teachers were requested to show their perception with a five point scale. The qualitative approach included semi-structured interview with teachers. The data findings were presented in statistical and descriptive manner considering various aspects of teaching profession. Literature review from different articles and books were helpful to develop ideas regarding key aspects of teaching profession and teachers' satisfaction and dissatisfaction. Literature was also helpful to construct idea for developing tools and data analysis.

3.2 Area of the study

The study was carried out purposively in 10 schools of Dhaka and Gazipur district. The schools were selected from both government and non-government type.

School Type	District		Total
	Dhaka	Gazipur	
Government	3	1	4
Non-Government	2	4	6
Total	5	5	10

Table 3.1: Study Area

3.3 Sample of the study

For collecting data 20 Social Science teachers were selected from 10 schools purposively. Among the teachers 8 were male and 12 were female. As the study investigated Social Science teachers' professional perception; key issues like training, initiatives for students' results, teaching aids and materials, students' achievement evaluation, responsibility, school environment, school administration, scope and their professional opportunities etc. were discussed with the teachers.

District	Respondents for the study		Total
	Govt. School	Non-Govt. School	
Dhaka	3x2=6	2x2=4	10
Gazipur	1x2=2	4x2=8	10
Total	8	12	20

Table 3.2: Sampling Design

3.4 Description of tools

In order to maintain the validity of data two types of data collection instruments were used to examine the perception of secondary school Social Science teachers about their profession. In each tool factors related with teachers' role, opportunity, satisfaction and dissatisfaction were set to find out their real view.

Opinionnaire

20 Items opinionnaire were developed to gather quantitative data regarding professional satisfaction and key elements of profession. In this tool, there were five response alternatives provided for each item, with differential weights assigned as 5= strongly agree, 4= agree, 3= cursorily agree, 2= neutral, and 1= disagree. Higher scores indicate a greater significance for the item measured.

Interview schedule

Total 41 items were developed for Interview schedule which was divided into two parts. General information about the respondent like name of the teacher, name of the school, type of the school, address, birth place of the teacher, classes involved in teaching, subjects of teaching, major subject of teaching, salary of the teacher, others facility, years of experience, educational qualifications and professional training were collected in the first part. Second part was developed to collect detail and descriptive information for the study. Only 5 items were structured in this portion and other 22 items were open-ended. For the open-ended items I encouraged teachers to express their opinion and views as they think about their profession.

3.5 Data collection procedure

The data collection was held at the selected schools with direct participation of me. Tools were piloted in a school at Dhaka. As my supervisor gave suggestion for several times at the time of tool construction, tools were found okay when I performed field-testing. At first I collect data from Gazipur then Dhaka. Though I went to schools at working days I need to go some schools for several days. At the time of collecting data firstly, I encouraged teachers to response by describing the objectives and perspectives of my study. Secondly, I supplied opinionnaire to them to response by them. Thirdly, I encourage them to response in a face to face interview. Most of the teachers I met were helpful and friendly to deliver each and every item of two tools though they had a great business.

3.6 Techniques of data analysis

Different themes related to teachers' profession was identified and data were analyzed under each theme. This study employed SPSS-16.0 for analyzing the data collected through the survey opinionnaire and performed the statistical analysis. Simple percentages and correlation of respondents against the supplied evidence were computed for opinionnaire survey. In this case, I consider types of school, teachers' birth place, major subject of teaching, gender and experience. For analyzing the data and evidence obtained from interview a descriptive approach was used. The quantitative data were shown in tables. Only percentile presentation was took place in those tables. The qualitative data was sorted out according to the emerged themes, concepts. In some cases statistical analysis were performed for the data collected through interview schedule gathering those in common theme.

3.7 Limitations of the study

To develop a concept about Social Science teachers' perception about their profession is very important for related persons and organizations. By understanding teachers' perception policy makers, teacher educator, curriculum related authority, related organizations and persons will be able to take right decision for teachers' best performance through proper satisfaction. Due to my limitation of time and money I collected data from Social Science teachers of two districts; it would be more reliable if it was collected from every district of Bangladesh. To understand various aspects of Social Science teachers' profession teacher educators, other subject teachers, students and head teachers' information could make realistic conclusion for this study. So, one of the important limitations of this study was not selecting these group as sample. In this research information was collected from teachers through interview and opinionnaire. But observation of teachers' class room activities and daily life would be the best way to make the study more authentic.

Chapter Four

Data Analysis and Interpretation

The study was conducted to understand Social Science teachers' perception about teaching profession. For this reason data and information were collected from Social Science teachers of secondary schools. Though samples were selected purposively, total 20 teachers of government and non-government schools were selected from Dhaka and Gazipur Districts to know their real opinion. To maintain the validity, data and information were collected through interview schedule and opinionnaire from each respondent. To conduct statistical interpretation, data collected through interview schedule were classified regarding respondents' opinion. SPSS-16.0 was employed to conduct simple statistical analysis like; frequencies, percentage, Mean, Standard Deviation and cross tabulation for collected data from both interview schedule and opinionnaire. To make the analyzed data visible and easily understandable MS Excel-2003 & 2007 were employed to develop figures. In this chapter data analysis and interpretation are done on the basis of different aspects of teaching profession and situation of teachers i.e. gender, educational qualification, professional training, salary, birth place, years of teaching experience and so on.

Among the interviewed teachers 100 % were involved in Social Science teaching though most of them had classes in other subjects i.e. Bangla (55%), English (45%), Agriculture (5%), Civics (10%), Religious Studies (15%), General Science (20%), Computer (5%), Mathematics (10%), History (5%), Economics (5%) and Geography (5%). On the other hand all teachers (100%) conducted class in grade IX or X while they also have to conduct class in other grades at secondary level. As the respondents had a variety of responsibility and experience, this was a huge opportunity for this study to find out their perception about their profession.

Table 4.1 gives an idea about major influence on teachers to take teaching as their profession. About one-third (30 %) teachers told that they involved in this profession from the necessity of job. Describing teaching as a great and dignified profession 25 % teachers said, this was the reason of their involvement. Though 10 % is not very significant figure but this percent came from two female teachers who think that this is the best profession for women while 'serve the nation by participating in building up good citizen' and 'disseminate achieved knowledge to the students' told by respectively 20 % and 15 % teachers.

Level	Response	Frequency	Percent
Major influence to take teaching as profession	Necessity of job	6	30
	Serve the nation by participating in building up good citizen	4	20
	Disseminate achieved knowledge to the students	3	15
	Best profession for the women	2	10
	Great and dignified profession	5	25
Specialty of teaching profession than other professions	An honest and great profession to build up nation and social welfare	14	70
	No specialty and less honor	3	15
	Secured than other profession	3	15

Table 4.1: Influence to involve in teaching and Specialty of teaching profession

Though teachers express various reasons for choosing this profession 70% teachers distinguish this profession from other profession for an honest and great profession to build up nation and scope of social welfare. Some teachers (15 %) told about security than other profession while 15 % find out no specialty and less honor (table 4.1). About teaching

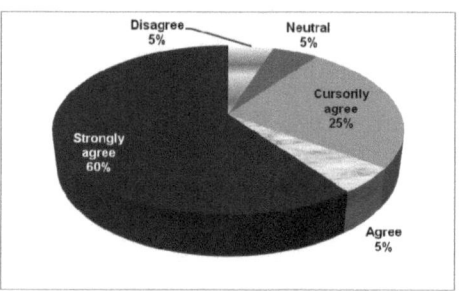

Figure 4.1: Teaching profession is the best profession

profession teachers express their views in the opinionnaire. The mean of their view is 4.10, which expose that teachers' view about 'teaching profession as best' is 82%, where 60 % teachers were strongly agreed in their opinions (figure 4.1).

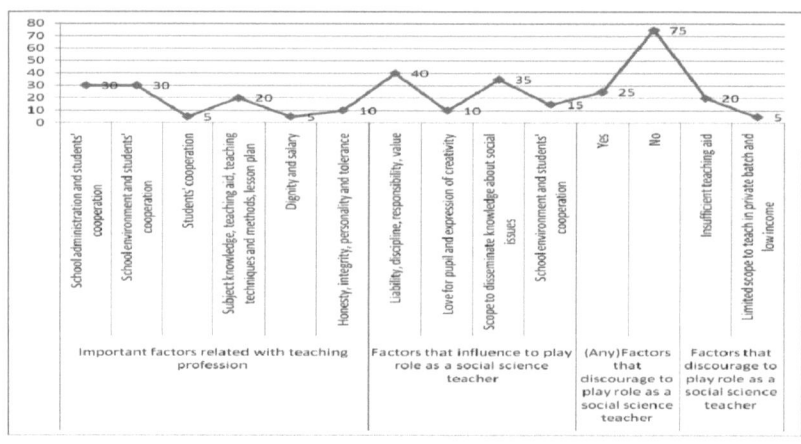

Figure 4.2: Factors of teaching profession

To identify factors related with teaching profession interviewed teachers mentioned various factors (figure 4.2). In those factors school administration, school environment, students' cooperation, subject knowledge, teaching aids, teaching methods and techniques got most importance. But 40 % teachers highlight liability, integrity, responsibility and value as influencing factor to play role as a Social Science teachers, though they did not mention these as factors related with teaching profession. About one-third (35 %) teachers talked about scope to disseminate knowledge about social issues while 15 % school environment and students' cooperation as influential factors for their profession. Figure 4.2 also illustrate that 75% teachers found no factor that discourage them to perform in teaching profession. Among the 25 % teachers who told about discouraging factors, 20 % mentioned insufficient teaching aid and 5 % talked about limited scope to teach in private batch and low income.

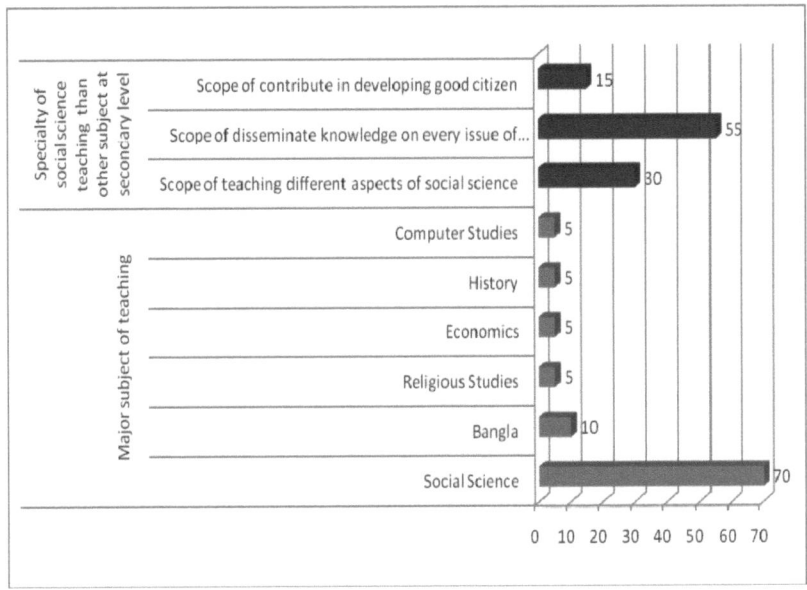

Figure 4.3: Teachers' view on specialty of Social Science teaching and major subject of teaching

Figure 4.3 shows that 55 % teachers find out specialty of Social Science teaching than other subject at secondary level for the scope of disseminate knowledge on every issue of the society. In this regard only 15 % teachers talked about the sope of contribution in developing good citizen though 70 % teachers had Social Science as their major subject of teaching. Some teachers (40%) strongly agreed that they enjoy Social Science more than teaching other subject (figure 4.4). In this regard Mean of teachers' opinion is 4.20 and Standerd Daviation is 0.77 which express teachers' enjoyment for Social Science teaching. While 55 % teachers find out specialty of Social Science teaching than other subject (figure 4.3), though delivering knowledge is major responsibility of a teacher it should not be considered as specialty, 50 % teacher mentioned that they express their specialty through delivering basic social knowledge to the students (figure 4.4). Figure 4.4 also illustrates many way followed by teachers to express their specialty i.e. usuing perfect teaching aids, information and examples (30 %), reading more books about this subject (10 %) and influencieng students about social organization and co-curricular activities (5%).

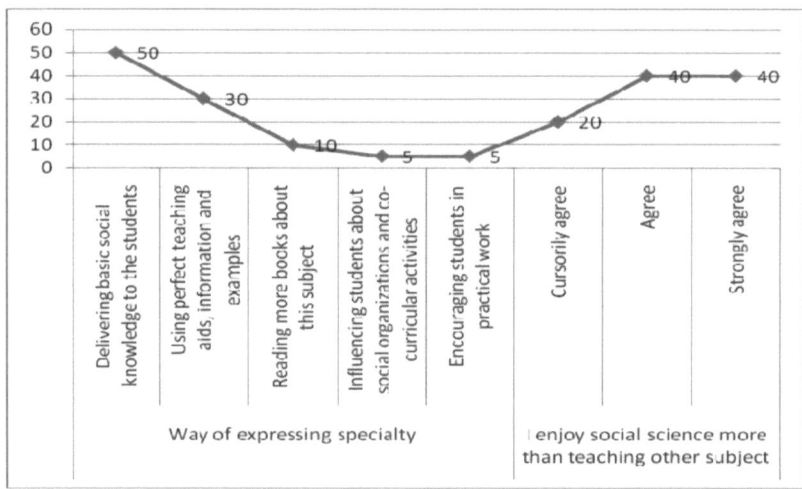

Figure 4.4: Enjoyment of Social Science teaching and way of expressing specialty

Average 6 classes were conducted by 40 % teachers daily, while 5, 4 and 3 classes were conducted respectively by 35 %, 20 % and 5 % teachers. On the other hand, 40% teachers express that if they conduct average 4 classes daily effective teaching could be ensured. To conduct daily 3 classes supported by 35 % and 2 classes by 20% teachers (figure 4.5).

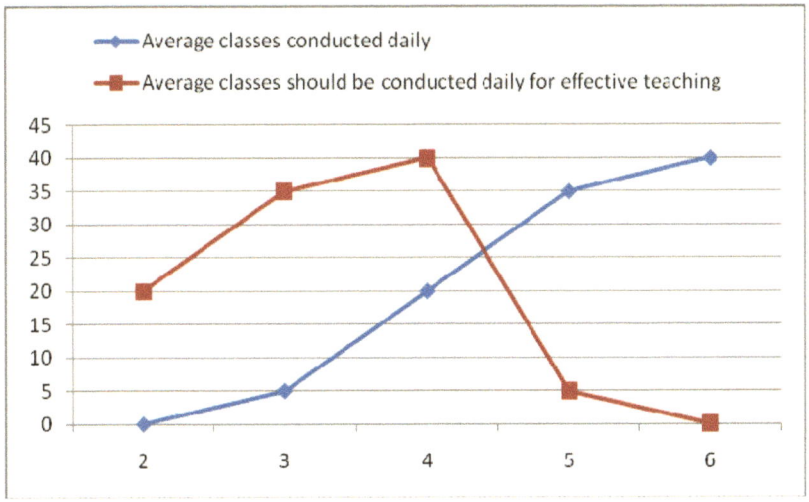

Figure 4.5: Average classes should be conducted for effective teaching

All interviewed teachers (100 %) told that training can help them especially in teaching Social Science. Figure 4.6 presents teachers' view about training those can help them in teaching Social Science and their opinion about received training for teaching this subject. In this regard 50 % teachers support TQI and 15 % teachers support effective teaching learning oriented training. Subject based training, teaching aid development training and modern need based teaching learning & teaching aid oriented training were support by 10 % teachers. On the other hand, 35 % teachers disagreed in the opinion of getting necessery training for Social Science teaching.

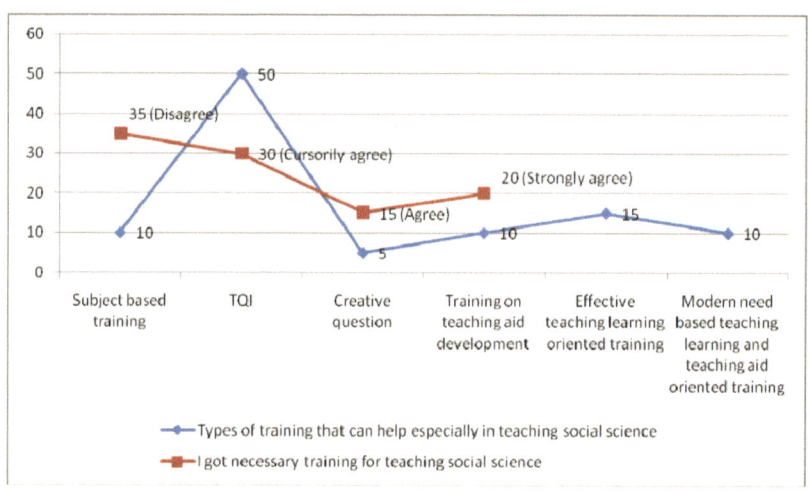

Figure 4.6: Helpful and received training for teaching Social Science

Mean of teachers' opinion about receiving necessary training is 2.85 and standard deaviation is 1.56. Calculated Mean expresses that teachers did not get necessary training for Social Science teaching and standard deviation also expresses significant difference among teachers' opinion.

Level	Response	Frequency	Percent
Effective measures for students doing good result in Social Science	Teaching with sufficient teaching aid	5	25
	Group discussion and assignment	3	15
	Field trip	2	10
	Regular examination	5	25
	More study and practice	3	15
	Student oriented teaching	1	5
	SBA	1	5
Types of measures taken for students good result	Class test	9	45
	Developing and conserving teaching aids by students	3	15
	Assignment and group discussion	2	10
	Use of subject based teaching aids	6	30

Table 4.2: Effective and Taken Measures for Students good result

Table 4.2 shows that 25 % teachers mentioned teaching with sufficient teaching aid and regular examination as effective measures for students; doing good result in

Social Science. A little number of teachers (15 %) gave importance on more study & practice and group discussion and assignment in this regard. In the interview 95 % teachers told that they take measures for good result and in the opinionnaire 30 % teachers strongly agreed and 50 % agreed that they can take necessary measures for students' good results in Social Science (figure 4.7). Data collected from both tool almost express the same view of teachers about taking measures for good result. Teachers also mentioned various type of measures which are taken by them (table 4.2). Only 'assignment and group discussion' is found as 'effective measure' and 'taken by teachers' in the table 4.2. 45 % teachers told that they follow class test while 30 % use subject based teaching aids and 15 % develop & conserve teaching aids by students for good results in Social Science though these measures are not mentioned as effective for good result.

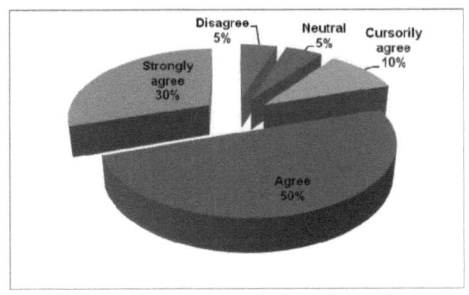

Figure 4.7: Taking necessary measures for good results in Social Science

The entire interviewed teachers mentioned map, picture, chart and globe as especial materials for presenting subject matter of Social Science. Whilst 91 % teachers point out that- books and other materials can play important role to ensure effective teaching, 52 % teachers agreed that they get supplementary books and others material from school library. Figure 4.8 also expresses the reverse order of teachers' opinion about necessity and availability of books and supplementary materials. One-fifth teachers (20 %) strongly agreed that they get opportunity to inform about contemporary social issues from different source and 30% teachers strongly agreed that to present Social Science subject matter they can use necessary aids (figure 4.8). Calculated Mean of these two items are 3.3 and 3.7 which express that teachers were cursorily agreed with these items.

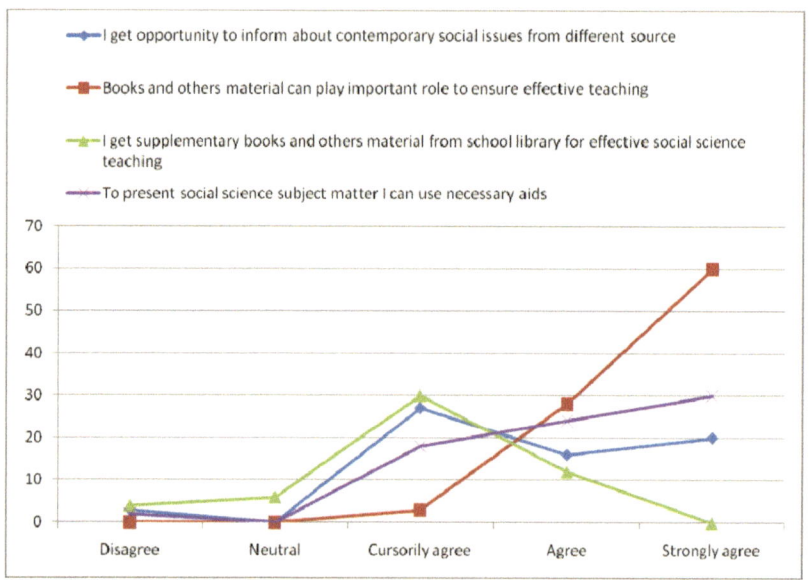

Figure 4.8: Opinion about teaching aids and instructional materials

Figure 4.9 illustrates teachers' view about students' evaluation methods that should be followed especially for Social Science subject. In this regard 40 % teachers support assignment and participation in practical work. On the other hand 30% teachers support evaluation methods which are now

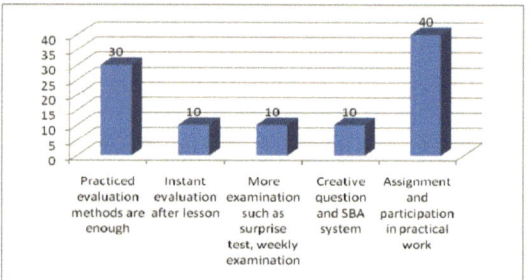

Figure 4.9: Students' evaluation methods in Social Science

practiced. Small number teachers (10 %) express their view for continuous evaluation after lesson, more examination such as surprise test, weekly examination, creative question and SBA system. According to the teachers' opinion 78 % can follow appropriate methods for Social Science students' evaluation. Mean opinion of teachers is 3.55 for getting opportunity to use creative methods appropriately (figure 4.10). In this regard standard deviation is 1.36, i.e. few teachers got this opportunity. While to ensure effective teaching and evaluation 92 % teachers emphasis on to bring out students out of classroom, only 47 % teachers get opportunity to bring out students for teaching and evaluating as per necessity. Mean opinion and standard deviation for 'feeling needs' & 'getting opportunity' are respectively 4.6 & 2.35 and 0.68 & 1.53, i.e. the deviation among teachers for feeling needs is very low but a few teachers getting this opportunity (figure 4.10).

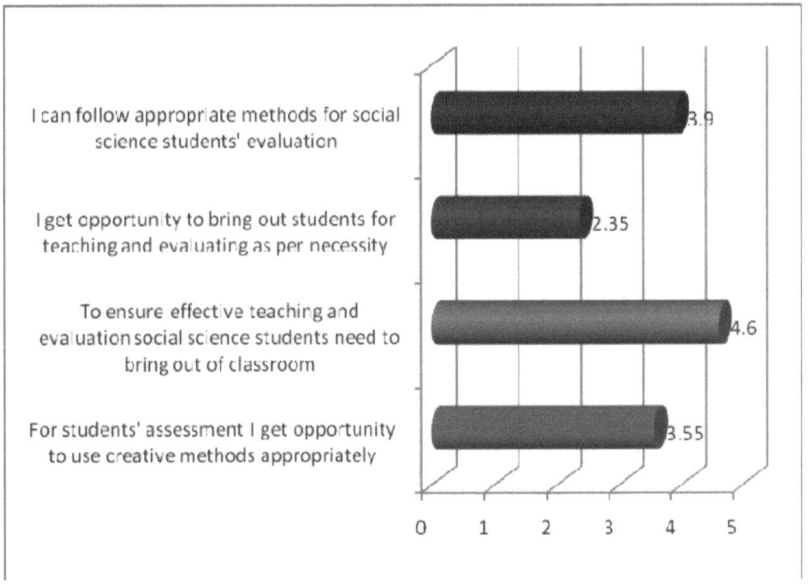

Figure 4.10: Opinion about effective teaching and assessment

Almost all Social Science teachers (95 %) think that they have various roles out of school. They mentioned various roles like- inform people about social issues, encourage people in tree plantation, students' home visit, arrange study tour and provide education to the illiterate and poor people. Among these roles 'inform people about social issues' got maximum (55 %) teachers' support as their role (figure 4.11).

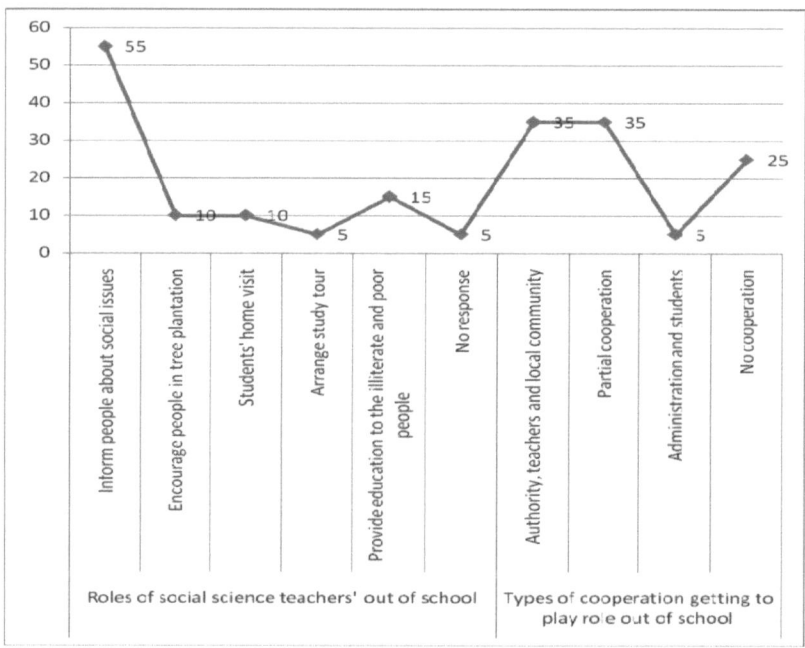

Figure 4.11: Roles 'out of school' and 'types of cooperation' to play role

To play role out of school 35 % teachers are getting cooperation of school authority, colleagues and local communities and the same percent teachers mentioned partial cooperation without mentioning types. One-fourth teachers (25 %) told that they do not get any cooperation while only 5 % teachers told about cooperation from administration and students (figure 4.11). Among the interviewed teachers the birth place of 9 teachers' was same and the rest 11 came from different Districts. Table

4.3 shows the response of teachers' about carrying out social responsibility in respective of their birth place. There is no significance difference between two categories of teachers in this respect.

Birth place of teacher	I also carry out various social responsibilities out of school					Total
	Disagree	Neutral	Cursorily agree	Agree	Strongly agree	
Same of the school	0	1	2	3	3	9
Different from the school	3	0	2	2	4	11
Total	3	1	4	5	7	20

Table 4.3: Relation with birth place and carrying out responsibilities out of school

As the Mean opinion of teachers is 3.6 and standard deviation is 1.43, it can be told that many teachers carry out various responsibilities out of school and there are significant differences among their opinions. But table 4.3 shows that this difference is not happened for the difference of their birth and school place and the average of the response of teachers from same district and different districts are 3.89 and 3.36.

Level	Response	Frequency	Percent
Factors of school environment	Physical facilities of school	10	50
	Play ground, garden	1	5
	Discipline and cleanliness	4	20
	School administration and teaching staff	3	15
	Student	2	10
Factor that help most to playing role	Students' cooperation	4	20
	School administration	10	50
	Teaching aids and materials	1	5
	Physical facilities of school	3	15
	Discipline	2	10
Factor that in-cooperate to playing role	Conduct class of other subjects	1	5
	Insufficient library, inadequate preservation system of teaching aids and small classroom	3	15
	In cooperation from teachers	1	5
	Unequal attitude of administration	1	5
	Political interfere	2	10
	Electricity problem	1	5
	Change of methods and techniques in education system	1	5
	No applicable	10	50

Table 4.4: Factors of school environment

Interviewed teachers identified physical facilities of school, play ground, garden, student, school administration, teaching staff, discipline, cleanliness, play ground and garden as factors of school environment (table 4.4). Among the teachers 50 % told that school administration help them most to play role as a Social Science teacher. One-fifth teachers (20 %) mentioned students' cooperation and 15 % talked about physical facilities of school as helping factors of school environment. Table 4.4 also shows that 50 % did not mention any factor that discourages them to do their job. Physical facilities like insufficient library, inadequate preservation system of teaching aids and small classroom are mentioned by 15 % teachers as discouraging factors and 10 % teachers talked about political interfere in this regard. Unequal attitude of administration in-cooperate 5 % teachers to play their role (table 4.4) on the other hand figure 4.12 illustrate support from school administration to accomplishing teachers' role. Figure 4.12 presents the comparison between government and non-government school teachers' opinion in this issue.

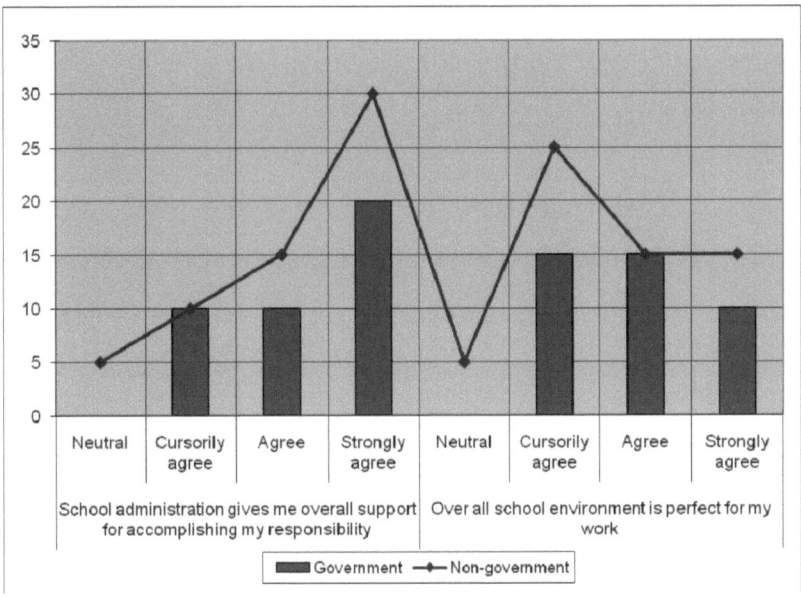

Figure 4.12: Support from school administration

The Mean opinion of teachers' about the support of school administration to do their work is 4.2 and standard deviation is 0.95. As the Mean is above 4 and standard deviation is below 1, it can be said that all of the teachers show a satisfactory feelings to school administrations cooperation. Figure 4.12 expresses that teachers of non-government schools are more satisfied than government schools as they are getting more support from school administration. Figure also expresses that school environment of non-government schools are better than government schools to accomplishing teachers responsibility.

	There are sufficient scopes in my school for professional development as a Social Science teacher					Total
Type of school	Disagree	Neutral	Cursorily agree	Agree	Strongly agree	
Government	2	1	1	2	2	8
Non-government	2	0	6	2	2	12
Total	4	1	7	4	4	20

Table 4.5: Scope of professional development

Table 4.5 shows the cross tabulation of types of schools and scope of teachers' professional development. From the table it can be said that there are no significant difference between government and non-government schools regarding scopes of teachers' professional development. But the Mean opinion of teachers about this issue is 3.15 which express that teachers of government and non-government schools have a limited scope for professional development.

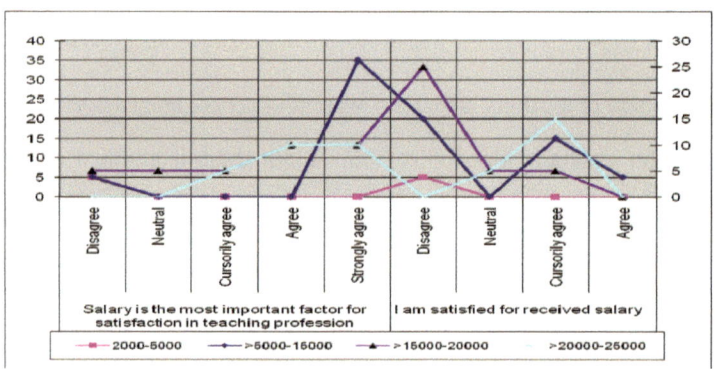

Figure 4.13: Importance and satisfaction for salary

Figure 4.13 shows that the teachers who received salary 2000-5000 BDT have no feelings about salary. They neither considered salary as the most important factor nor showed satisfaction for received salary. The same case is also applicable for the highest salary receiver group with a little difference. But two groups who are belonging in the middle showed a reverse opinion. Among the teachers 35 % and 10% teachers of the salary range respectively >5000-15000 and >15000-20000 were strongly agreed that salary is the most important factor for satisfaction in teaching profession. Both groups also told that they are dissatisfied for received salary respectively 20 % and 25 %. The mean opinion of teachers for received salary and others facility are 1.95 and 1.85 which express that teachers are not satisfied for their salary and others facility though 60% teachers told that they are receiving other facilities.

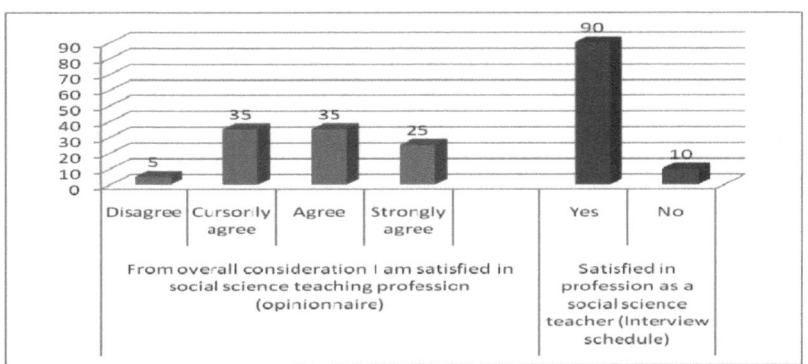

Figure 4.14: Satisfaction in teaching profession as a Social Science teacher

Figure 4.14 illustrates 90 % Social Science teachers told that they are satisfied and their Mean opinion is 3.75 i.e. 75 % teachers mentioned that they are satisfied in teaching profession. In this situation they mentioned almost the same reason of involving in this profession. Near about half of the teachers (45 %) are satisfied in this profession because they can perform to develop perfect citizen and 20 % get pleasure by teaching Social Science. Two teachers (10%) mentioned less respect and limited financial facility for their dissatisfaction.

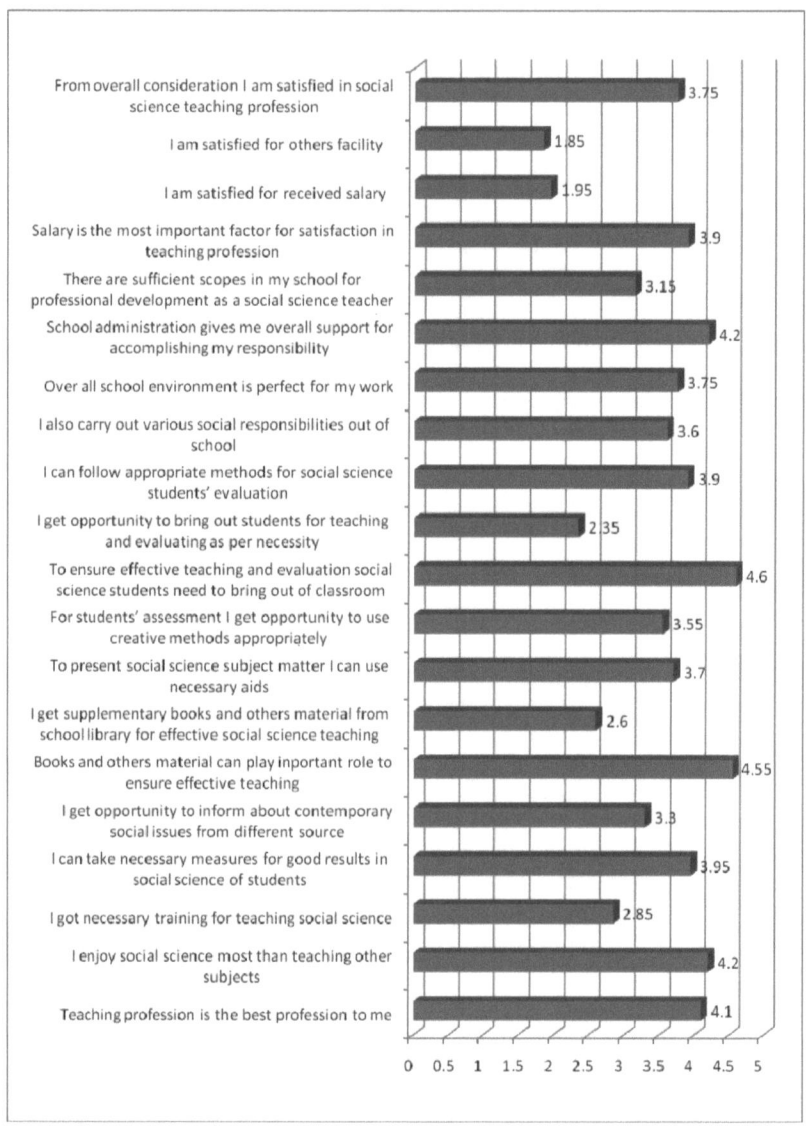

Figure 4.15: Mean of teachers' opinion about teaching profession

Figure 4.15 show that teachers are dissatisfied for received salary and others facilities. The height Mean opinion is expressed the needs for bring out Social Science students out of classroom for effective teaching and evaluation.

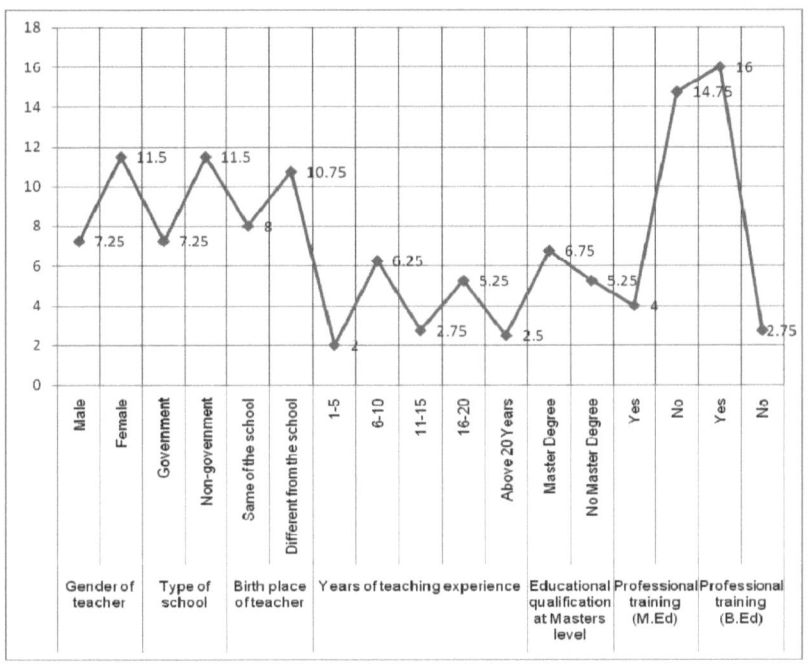

Figure 4.16: Satisfaction of Social Science teachers

Figure 4.16 illustrates the comparison among different variables and Satisfaction as a Social Science teacher which is developed from Average of responses in cross tabulations. Between male and female teachers females are more satisfied than male. Teachers of government schools are less satisfied than non-government and their Mean opinion are respectively 7.25 and 11.5. Teachers who came from different districts are more satisfied than those are local. Satisfaction in respect of teaching experience showed an irregular curve. Most junior and senior teachers are less satisfied than the teachers of 6-10 and 16-20 years experienced but middle aged teachers are also less satisfied. Teachers who had Master Degree were showed their more satisfaction than who did not hold this. This trend is reverse for professional training i.e. who had M.Ed was less satisfied than B.Ed holders.

Chapter Five

Findings and Discussion

5.1 Findings

The study involved 8 (eight) Social Science teachers from government schools and 12 (twelve) from non-government schools. All of the interviewed teachers are involved in Social Science teaching while 70 % had this subject as major. Majority of the teachers had experience of several years. All of the teachers had Bachelor Degree and 14 of them (70%) had Master Degree while 17 (seventeen) had B.Ed and 4 (four) had M.Ed Degree. According Husain (2004) for proper perception knowledge and experience are very important. Kochhar (1983) also suggested some qualities which Social Science teachers should have. As the interviewed teachers were from different types of institutions and had variety of educational qualification and experience, their opinion and views may reflect perfect perception of Social Science teachers' about teaching profession in this study. The findings drawn from the teachers' opinion and interview are stated below:

5.1.1 Among the interviewed teachers 30 % involved in teaching profession from the necessity of job. In the same way Oplataka (2007) characterized teaching in terms of knowledge transmission, adherence to prescribed curriculum and textbooks, summative assessment of student achievements, and conservativeness. One-fourth (25 %) teachers mentioned this profession great and dignified while 20 % talked about the scope of serves the nation by participating in building up good citizen as the major influence to take teaching as profession. On the other hand 60 % teachers opined that teaching is the best profession. Labrana (2007) find out that the main motivation of teachers to take this profession was to disseminate knowledge to students and in this study 15 % teachers mentioned the same reason in this regard.

5.1.2 School administration, students' cooperation, subject knowledge, teaching aid, teaching techniques & methods, lesson plan, honesty, integrity, personality, tolerance, dignity and salary were important factors to the teachers related with teaching profession. Gonzalez, Brown and Slate (2008) find out salary, teacher education program, student discipline, feed back from school administration and educational resource which are very important for teachers regarding their profession. In this issue Raju and Srivastava (1994) mentioned work related personality, perceived status, interest in profession, intrinsic motivation, social support and positive group attitudes. MCEETYA (2003) also illustrate professional elements incorporating professional knowledge, practice, value and relationship in a framework. To the teachers' liability, discipline, responsibility, value, scope to disseminate knowledge about social issues, school environment, love for pupil and expression of creativity are important factors to play role as a Social Science teacher. Though 75 % mentioned there are no factors that discourage them in this regard, insufficient teaching aid, limited scope to teach in private batch and low income are discouraging factors to some teachers.

5.1.3 Scope of disseminate knowledge to the students on every issue of the society is the main specialty of Social Science teaching to the teachers. Scope of teaching for different aspects of Social Science and contributing in developing good citizen are also important specialty of teaching this subject. In this respect Kochhar (1983) called Social Science teacher a scientist as well as an artist. As most of the teachers enjoy teaching Social Science than other subject, they express their specialty through delivering basic social knowledge to the students, using perfect teaching aids, information and examples and influencing students about social organizations and co-curricular activities. Wade (1995) also found Social Science teachers in a unique position to giving their students opportunities for active involvement in the community and the world.

5.1.4 Among the teachers 40 % conducted 6 classes and 35 % conducted 5 classes per day. Among them 40 % suggested 4 classes and 35 % suggested 3 classes for making teaching effective. Whitehead (2009) also suggested for alleviate teacher stress. But Perrachione, Rosser and Petersen (2008) did not found relationship between satisfaction with the job of teaching and work-related duties.

5.1.5 Social Science teachers strongly agreed that training can help them in teaching this subject but they are not receiving proper training in this regard. Subject based in-service training, modern need based teaching-learning oriented training and training on teaching aid & evaluation are very necessary for them. According to Raju and Srivastava (1994) perceived advancement and desire to improve skills for professional purpose discriminated more or less committed teachers. Oplatka (2007) find out that in developing countries teachers seek constantly escape for limited opportunities to participate in in-service training.

5.1.6 Maximum teachers are taking necessary measures for students' good result in Social Science. Though teachers mentioned teaching with sufficient teaching aid, regular examination, group discussion & assignment, field trip, student oriented teaching and SBA as effective for students doing good result in this subject, majority of them followed class test and use of subject based teaching aids. On the other hand Waid and Mcnergney (2003) found that teachers can improve student achievement when they communicate high expectations, avoid criticism, reward truly praiseworthy behavior, and provide abundant opportunities for success (academic learning time) on material over which students are tested.

5.1.7 According to teachers map, chart, picture and globe are especial materials for presenting subject matter of Social Science. Though maximum teachers think that books and supplementary materials can play important role to ensure effective teaching, many of them do not get those from school library. A few teachers have opportunity to inform contemporary social issues while a small number of teachers can use necessary aids to present Social Science subject matter. MCEETYA (2003) found that teachers communicate effectively with their students and establish clear goals for learning, inquiry techniques and teaching strategies, and use a range of tools, activities, and resources to engage their students in learning to organize the content in logical and structured way to meet learning goals.

5.1.8 For Social Science students evaluation teachers identified assignment, participation in practical work, instant evaluation after lesson, surprise test, weekly examination, creative question and SBA as effective ways. Majority of teachers claimed that they can follow appropriate evaluation methods for Social Science students' assessment. A few number of teachers got the opportunity to use creative assessment methods and a significant number of teachers support traditional evaluation methods while Occupational Outlook Handbook (2010-2011) asked to use new assessment methods.

5.1.9 Almost all of the teachers gave emphasis on brings out students out of classroom to ensure effective teaching and evaluation but a few teachers got the opportunity to do this as per necessity. Occupational Outlook Handbook (2010-2011) suggests teachers to oversee study halls and homerooms, supervise extracurricular activities, and accompany students on field trips for conducting classroom activities.

5.1.10 Majority of the Social Science teachers think that they have various roles out of school. Roles out of school like- inform people about social issues, encourage people in tree plantation, students' home visit, arrange study tour and provide education to the illiterate and poor people were mentioned by the teachers. Only a few teachers do not get any cooperation to play role out of school while maximum teachers got support from school authority, colleagues, local communities and school administration. There is no significant difference between the local teachers and the teachers from different districts regarding carrying out responsibility out of school. But Reed (2009) found that local teachers have a different relationship to the community than the other educators in the schools where they practice. Their ties to the community give them a particularized knowledge of the school's social and cultural context which helps them to play role out of school.

5.1.11 Teachers identified different factors of school environment, within those factors school administration help them most to play role as a Social Science teacher. Students' cooperation, physical facilities of school and discipline also help them in this regard. Though half of the teachers did not mentioned any factor that discourage them to play role, rest of them told about insufficient library, inadequate preservation system of teaching aids, small classroom, unequal attitude of school administration, political interfere, in-cooperation from colleagues, electricity problem as discouraging factors. Whitehead (2009) finds out overcrowding of classrooms and poor condition of school buildings for teachers' dissatisfaction in their profession. Huang and Waxman (2008) investigate teachers' perceptions about their school environments, especially in the areas of professional interest and staff freedom, were positively associated with their satisfaction. Several school environmental aspects influenced the total years they planned to teach and their intention to teach at the school. Earthman and Lemasters (2009) indicate that the physical environment of school influences attitudes of teachers, which in turn affects their productivity. Teachers also emphasized their satisfaction for interactions with students, relationships held with colleagues and opportunities to contribute to the growth of individuals and the development of society. Sources of dissatisfaction were social problems and their impact on teachers' work, students' lack of interest and bad behavior (Zembylas and Papanastasiou, 2006).

5.1.12 Teachers of non-government schools are more satisfied than government schools because they are getting more support from school administration. School environment of non-government schools are also better than government schools to accomplishing teachers work and responsibility. Though there is no significant difference between both types of schools in terms of teachers' professional development scope, both government and non-government schools have limited opportunity for teachers' professional development. Gonzalez, Brown and Slate (2008) find out school administration that is very important for teachers regarding their profession. Strong positive relationship was revealed to Cerit (2009) between servant leadership behaviors of school principals and teachers' job satisfaction and servant leadership was a significant predictor of teacher job satisfaction. Chi Keung (2008) mentioned that teacher participation in decision-making is one of the recommendations of school-based management and one of the key characteristics of an effective school. Huysman (2008) analyzed that the lowest ranked satisfaction dimensions were extrinsic satisfaction items which included compensation and school policies, advancement, and recognition. According to Zembylas and Papanastasiou (2006) sources of dissatisfaction were the centralized educational system and the lack of professional autonomy in schools, and teacher evaluation and promotion prospects.

5.1.13 Salary is one of the most important factor for satisfaction in teaching profession. Most of the teachers are not satisfied for received salary and others facilities. According to Gonzalez, Brown and Slate (2008) salary is the number one factor that is very important for teachers regarding their profession. On the other hand Cypriot teachers chose this career because of the salary, the hours, and the holidays associated with this profession (Zembylas and Papanastasiou, 2004). Many factors have been identified as influencing teacher professional satisfaction and retention, and salary is often at the top of the lists (Michael, 2006).

5.1.14 Maximum Social Science teachers are satisfied in teaching profession though a few teachers mention less respect and limited income for their dissatisfaction. According Saiti (2007) Job satisfaction is an important issue, but remains a complex one as it is difficult to measure. Job satisfaction and the teaching profession are highly associated, with an important aspect of quality education and teachers' perception about their profession. A wide range of factors such as the working environment, its manner of organization, demography and individual circumstances, etc., can substantially affect the level of job satisfaction attained by individuals. Between male and female teachers females are more satisfied than male. Teachers of government schools are less satisfied than non-government schools. Teachers who came from different districts are more satisfied than those are local. Teaching experience has no significant relation with teachers' job satisfaction. But Liu and Ramsey (2008) found that teachers were least satisfied with work conditions and compensation. They also found that teachers' job satisfaction varied with gender, years of teaching, and career status. Master Degree holder teachers are getting more satisfaction than who has only Bachelor Degree but M.Ed holders are less satisfied than B.Ed holders i.e. better professional degree may make more dissatisfaction to teachers as they are not getting better facilities.

5.2 Discussion

5.2.1 As teaching profession is not only an occupation but has a great responsibility to the society, concern authority should take proper initiative to encourage qualified young generation to take this profession form its expectation not only for necessity of job.

5.2.2 For better performance of Social Science teachers work load or number of classes should be balanced with their capacity of completing daily responsibility. Social Science teachers also should not be engage to conduct classes of other subjects if they do not want to do so.

5.2.3 Social Science teachers should have opportunity to participate in-service training for upgrading their teaching and evaluating capacity. Modern need based teaching-learning oriented training and training on teaching aid development & creative assessment should be incorporated in in-service training.

5.2.4 Maximum teachers are following traditional way for increasing students' achievement. Proper training on students psychology, appropriate teaching aids, freedom of implementing teaching methods should be provide to all Social Science teachers so that they could be able to do the perfect work for increasing students' achievement level.

5.2.5 Social Science teachers are using common and few teaching aids because of limited scope to inform contemporary social issues and get necessary materials from school library and school compound. Necessary measures should be taken to improve capacity of school library for contemporary information access and teaching aids development.

5.2.6 Although teachers claimed that they are following appropriate evaluation method for students' assessment, they should have the opportunity to inform new assessment methods and to implement those.

5.2.7 A few teachers getting the opportunity to bring out students out of school as per necessity for effective teaching and evaluation though almost all of the teachers' emphasis on this issue. So Social Science teachers should have opportunity and facility to follow the right way of teaching and evaluating this subject.

5.2.8 As majority teachers feel their responsibility out of school and can do the necessary job in this regard, proper training and facilities should be given for carry on their responsibility as well as increasing their feelings.

5.2.9 Factors of school environment those discourage Social Science teachers to accomplish their responsibility should be improve. In this regard concern authority should take initiative for insufficient library, inadequate preservation system of teaching aids, small classroom, unequal attitude of school administration, political interfere, colleague relation and electricity problem.

5.2.10 Support of government school administration to the Social Science teachers and elements of school environment should be improved. Both government and non-government school should increase scopes of professional development for Social Science teachers.

5.2.11 Most of the teachers are not satisfied for received salary and other facilities and salary is one of the most important factors for satisfaction in teaching profession to the teachers. So, proper initiative should be taken to ensure teachers professional satisfaction through salary and other facilities.

5.2.12 To encourage teachers to improve their teaching quality, professional qualification and other qualities should be evaluated and provision should be taken to provide better facilities for those, who hold better Degree.

Reference

Aggarwal, J. C. (1993). *Teaching of Social Studies.* Vikas Publishing House Pvt. Ltd. New Delhi.

Aggarwal, J. C. (2005). *Essentials of Educational Technology: Teaching Learning Innovations in Education.* Vikas Publishing House Pvt. Ltd. New Delhi.

Berwick, D. M. (2008). *The Epitaph of Profession.* Advance online publication. Retrieved from www.Bigp_08_JohnHuntLecture_Berwic_AOP.pdf

Brown, S. & Lent, R. (1996). A Social Cognitive Framework for Career Choice Counseling. *The Career Development Quarterly*, 44, 355-367. Retrieved from www.uky.edu/Education/EDP/.../learning_Social%20Cognitive.ppt

Buckley, J.W. & Buckley, M.H. (1974): *The Accounting Profession.* Melville: Los Angeles.

Bullock, A. & Trombley, S. (1999). *The New Fontana Dictionary of Modern Thought.* London: Harper-Collins.

Bureau of Labor Statistics (2008). *Occupational Outlook Handbook, 2008-09.* Teachers: Preschool, Kindergarten, Elementary, Middle, and Secondary. U.S. Department of Labor. Retrieved from http://www.bls.gov/oco/ocos069.htm

Bureau of Labor Statistics (2010). *Occupational Outlook Handbook*, 2010-11. Teachers—Kindergarten, Elementary, Middle, and Secondary. United States Department of Labor. Retrieved from http://www.bls.gov/oco/ocos318.htm

Cerit, Y. (2009). The Effects of Servant Leadership Behaviours of School Principals on Teachers' Job Satisfaction. *Educational Management Administration & Leadership.* 37 (5), 600-623. Retrieved from ema.sagepub.com/cgi/content/short/37/5/600

Cheng, C. K. (2008). The Effect of Shared Decision-Making on the Improvement in Teachers' Job Development . *New Horizons in Education.* 56 (3), 31-46. Retrieved from repository.ied.edu.hk/dspace/bitstream/2260.2/9275/1/9275.htm

Cook, L. A. & Cook, E. F. (1960). *A Sociological Approach to Education.* McGraw-Hill Books Company, Inc. New York.

Denton, E.M. (2009). Teachers' Perceptions of How the Leadership Styles and Practices of Principals Influence Their Job Satisfaction and Retention. Retrieved from http://digitalcommons.liberty.edu/cgi/viewcontent.cgi?article=1226&context=doctoral

Desimone, L.M. (2009). Improving Impact Studies of Teachers' Professional Development: Toward Better Conceptualizations and Measures. *Educational Researcher.* 38 (3), 81-199. Retrieved from http://edr.sagepub.com/cgi/content/abstract/38/3/181

Earthman, G.I. & Lemasters, L. K. (2009). Teacher Attitudes about Classroom Conditions. *Journal of Educational Administration.* 47 (3), 323-335. Emerald Group Publishing Limited. Retrieved from http://www.emeraldinsight.com/10.1108/09578230910955764

England, G.C. (1973). Impact of the Inspectorial System: A Profession Demeaned? *Journal of Educational Administration.* 11 (1), 43-49. MCB UP Ltd. Retrieved from http://www.emeraldinsight.com/10.1108/eb009686

Fry, S. W. (2008). On Borrowed Time: How Four Elementary Pre-service Teachers Learned to Teach Social Studies in the NCLB Era. Boise State University. Retrieved from http://www.socstrp.org/issues/getfile.cfm?volID=5&IssueID=10&ArticleID=138

Gaiser, R. R. (2009). The Teaching of Professionalism during Residency: Why It Is Failing and a Suggestion to Improve Its Success. *Economics, Education, and Policy.* Retrieved from http://www.anesthesiaandanalgesia.org/cgi/content/abstract/108/3/948

Gibson, D. W. (1965). *Social Perspectives on Education.* John Willy & Sons. New York.

Gimbert, B. G., Cristol, D. & Sene, A. M. (2007). The Impact of Teacher Preparation on Student Achievement in Algebra in a "Hard-to-Staff" Urban PreK-12-University Partnership. *School Effectiveness and School Improvement.* 18 (3), 245-272. Retrieved from www.informaworld.com/smpp/.../content~db=all~content=a779761446

Grossman, P. et al. (2009). Teaching Practice: A Cross-Professional Perspective. *Teachers College Record.* 111 (9). Retrieved from http://www.tcrecord.org/Content.asp?ContentID=15018

Hossain, N. (2009). School Exclusion as Social Exclusion: The Practices and Effects of a Conditional Cash Transfer Programme for the Poor in Bangladesh. Chronic Poverty Research Centre. Institute of Development Studies University of Sussex.

Huang, L.H. and Waxman, H.C. (2008). The Association of School Environment to Student Teachers' Satisfaction and Teaching Commitment. Retrieved from http://www.sciencedirect.com/science?_ob=ArticleURL&_udi=B6VD8-4TG28Y9-1&_user=10&_rdoc=1&_fmt=&_orig=search&_sort=d&_docanchor=&view=c&_searchStrId=1013618029&_rerunOrigin=scholar.google&_acct=C000050221&_version=1&_urlVersion=0&_userid=10&md5=984ea29709304781e02113cc82542f86

Husain, M.D. (2004). *Behavioral Science*. Scientific Media Services. Dhaka.

Huysman, J. T. (2008). Rural Teacher Satisfaction: An Analysis of Beliefs and Attitudes of Rural Teachers' Job Satisfaction. *Rural Educator.* 29 (2), 31-38. Retrieved from www.eric.ed.gov/ERICWebPortal/recordDetail?accno=EJ869291

Johnson, L. S. (2009). School Contexts and Student Belonging: A Mixed Methods Study of an Innovative High School. *Academic Development Institute.* V.19. Retrieved from http://www.adi.org/journal

Karakus, M. & Aslan, B. (2009). Teachers' Commitment Focuses: A Three-Dimensioned View. *Journal of Management Development.* 28 (5), 425-438. Emerald Group Publishing Limited. Retrieved from http://www.emeraldinsight.com/10.1108/02621710910955967

Klassen, R. M. & Anderson, C. J. K. (2009). How Times Change: Secondary Teachers' Job Satisfaction and Dissatisfaction in 1962 and 2007. *British Educational Research Journal.* 35 (5), 745-759. Retrieved from www.informaworld.com/.../content~content=a909483742~db=all~jumptype=rss

Kochhar.S.K. (1983). Teaching of social studies. S.K. Ghai. New Delhi.

Labrana and Munoz, C. (2007). History and Social Science Teachers' Perceptions of Their Profession: A Phenomenological Study. *Social Studies.* 98 (1), 20-24. Heldref Publications. Retrieved from http://www.heldref.org

Liu, X. S. & Ramsey, J. (2008). Teachers' Job Satisfaction: Analyses of the Teacher Follow-Up Survey in the United States for 2000-2001. *Teaching and Teacher Education.* 24 (5), 1173-1184. Retrieved from www.eric.ed.gov/ERICWebPortal/recordDetail?accno=EJ794701

Mau, W.J., Ellsworth, R. & Hawley, D. (2008). Job Satisfaction and Career Persistence of Beginning Teachers. *International Journal of Educational Management.* 22 (1), 48-61, Retrieved from www.emeraldinsight.com/Insight/viewContentItem.do;jsessionid...

MCEETYA (2003). *A National Framework for Professional Standards for Teaching.* Teacher quality and educational leadership Taskforce ministerial council on education. Employment Training and Youth Affairs. Retrieved from www.curriculum.edu.au/verve/_.../national_framework_file.pdf

Nelica L.G. (2008). Social Cognitive Approaches. Centre for Training in Career Guidance. School of Psychology. University of East London. Retrieved from http://www.guidance-research.org/EG/impprac/ImpP2/new-theories/social-cognitive

Oplatka, I. (2007).The Context and Profile of Teachers in Developing Countries in the Last Decade: A Revealing Discussion for Further Investigation. *International Journal of Educational Management.* 21 (6), 476-490. Emerald Group Publishing Limited. Retrieved from http://www.emeraldinsight.com/10.1108/09513540710780019

Perks, R.W.(1993). *Accounting and Society.* London: Chapman & Hall.

Perrachione, B. A., Rosser, V. J. & Petersen, G. J. (2008). Why Do They Stay? Elementary Teachers' Perceptions of Job Satisfaction and Retention. *Professional Educator.* 32 (2). Retrieved from www.eric.ed.gov/ERICWebPortal/recordDetail?accno

R. Krishnaveni, J. Anitha (2007). Educators' Professional Characteristics. *Quality Assurance in Education.* 15 (2), 149 – 161. Emerald Group Publishing Limited. Retrieved from www.emeraldinsight.com/10.1108/09684880710748910

Rahima C. W. (1995). Developing Active Citizens: Community Service Leaning in Social Studies Teacher Education. *Social Studies*. V.86. Retrieved from http://www.questia.com/googleScholar.qst;jsessionid=KzhG6JnwC8R9WXjwpPYZvYsQKJp1hJ1WppdZhWDntTnqrwJvwgTq!1273633868!-1334397701?docId=96246380

Reed, W.A. (2009) The Bridge is Built: The Role of Local Teachers in an Urban Elementary School. Retrieved from http://www.adi.org/journal/resources/SCJSpringSummer2009.pdf#page=59

Raju, P. M. & Srivastava, R.C. (1994). Factors Contributing to Commitment to the Teaching Profession. International Journal of Educational Management. 8 (5), 7 – 13. MCB UP Ltd. Retrieved from http://www.emeraldinsight.com/10.1108/09513549410065684

Rippon, J. H. (2005). Re-defining Careers in Education. *Career Development International*. 10 (4), 275 – 292. Emerald Group Publishing Limited. Retrieved from http://www.emeraldinsight.com/10.1108/13620430510609127

Saiti, A. (2007). Main Factors of Job Satisfaction among Primary School Educators: Factor Analysis of the Greek Reality. *Management in Education*. 21 (2), 28-32. Retrieved from www.eric.ed.gov/ERICWebPortal/recordDetail?accno=EJ803561

Skaalvik, E. M. & Skaalvik, S. (2009). Does School Context Matter? Relations with Teacher Burnout and Job Satisfaction. *Teaching and Teacher Education*. 25 (3), 518-524. Retrieved from *linkinghub.elsevier.com/retrieve/pii/S0742051X08002163*

Stronge, J. H. (2002). *Qualities of Effective Teachers*. Retrieved from http://zawodny.net/orientation/orientation%20odds%20and%20ends/The_Teacher_as_Person.pdf

The Center for the Future of Teaching and Learning (2009).*The Status of the Teaching Profession*. Santa Cruz. Retrieved from www.cftl.org

Wade, R.C .(1995). Developing Active Citizens: Community Service Leaning in Social Studies Teacher Education. *Social Studies*. Vl. 86. Retrieved from http://www.questia.com/googleScholar.qst;jsessionid=KzhG6JnwC8R9WXjwpPYZvYsQKJp1hJ1WppdZhWDntTnqrwJvwgTq!1273633868!-1334397701?docId=96246380

Waid, K. B. & Mcnergney (2003), R. F. Teacher - Responsibilities of Elementary and Secondary School Teachers, Qualifications of Elementary and Secondary Teachers. *Education Encyclopedia – State University.com* . Retrieved from http://education.stateuniversity.com/pages/2477/Teacher.html#ixzz0jCjCCjqi

Whitehead, D. P. (2009). Teacher, where Are You? *Childhood Education*. 85 (4). Retrieved from *www.eric.ed.gov/ERICWebPortal/recordDetail?accno=EJ840728*

Wong, C.; Wong, P.; Peng, K. Z. (2010). Effect of Middle-Level Leader and Teacher Emotional Intelligence on School Teachers' Job Satisfaction: The Case of Hong Kong. *Educational Management Administration & Leadership*. 38 (1). Retrieved from ema.sagepub.com/cgi/content/abstract/38/1/59

Zembylas, M. & Papanastasiou, M. (2004). Job Satisfaction Among School Teachers in Cyprus. *Journal of Educational Administration*. 42 (3), 357 – 374. Emerald Group Publishing Limited. Retrieved from http://www.emeraldinsight.com/10.1108/09578230410534676

Zembylas, M. & Papanastasiou, E. (2006). Sources of Teacher Job Satisfaction and Dissatisfaction in Cyprus. *Compare: A Journal of Comparative Education*. 36 (2), 229-247. Retrieved from www.informaworld.com/index/X7G406W114V24183.pdf